11542

P9-ELS-524

My Heart

Kathy Furgang

The Rosen Publishing Group

PowerKids Press™

New York

For Elizabeth

Published in 2001 by The Rosen Publishing Group, Inc.
29 East 21st Street, New York, NY 10010

First Edition

Book Design: Kim Sonsky

Illustration Credits: All organ 3-D illustrations © LifeArt/TechPool Studios, Inc.; All other 3-D illustrations by Kim Sonsky.

Furgang, Kathy.
  My heart / by Kathy Furgang.
    p. cm. — (My body)
  Includes index.
  Summary: Describes the parts, activities, and functions of the human heart and circulatory system and problems that may develop there.
  ISBN 0-8239-5574-5 (lib. bdg. : alk. paper)
  1. Heart—Juvenile literature. [1. Heart. 2. Blood. 3. Circulatory system.] I. Title.

QP111.6.F87 2000
612.1'7—dc21   99-088032

Manufactured in the United States of America

Contents

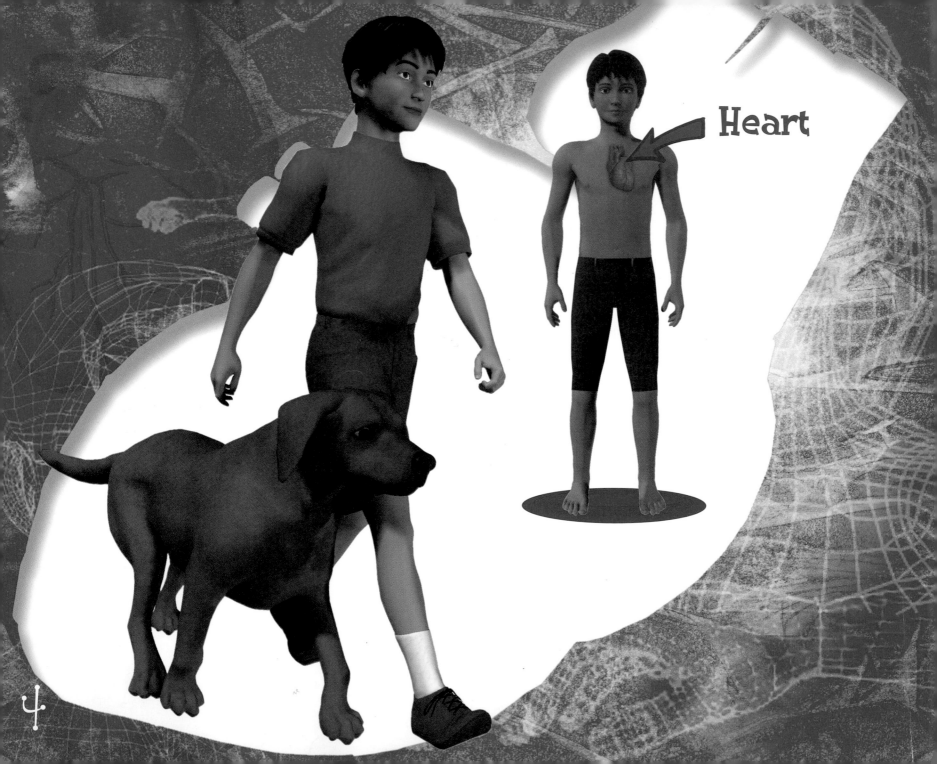

Heart

A Hardworking Pump

Inside your body there's an amazing pump called the heart. Your heart pumps blood to all parts of your body. You need blood to live. Blood carries the fuel your body needs to work. Your muscles need blood for energy so that you can be active and move around.

Your heart itself is a muscle. Each pump of blood into the body is one heartbeat. As long as you are alive, your heart will pump blood. The only time you could still be alive when your heart is not pumping is during a **heart transplant** or if you have an **artificial heart**.

Your heart is about the size of your fist. It is found in the middle of your chest and a little to the left side. Your heart beats about once every second while you are resting. When you exercise, it beats faster.

Help From Your Lungs

Each drop of blood brings your body a **gas** that you need to live. This gas is called **oxygen**. Oxygen is fuel that your body needs for energy. Once your body uses the oxygen, it creates another gas called **carbon dioxide**. These gases enter and leave your body through your lungs. Your lungs are two sacs in your chest that surround your heart. When you breathe in, your lungs suck in oxygen from the air. When you breathe out, your lungs also push out carbon dioxide. When your heart pumps blood to your lungs, carbon dioxide is removed from the blood, and oxygen is added.

Blood travels from your heart to your lungs so that oxygen can be added and carbon dioxide can be removed.

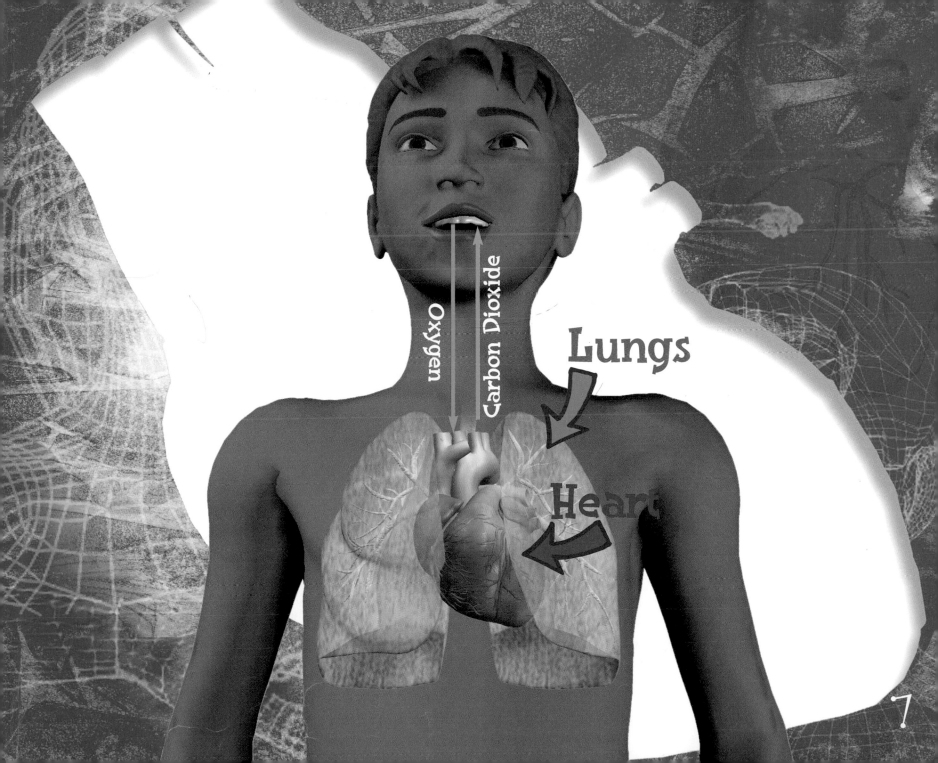

Oxygen

Carbon Dioxide

Lungs

Heart

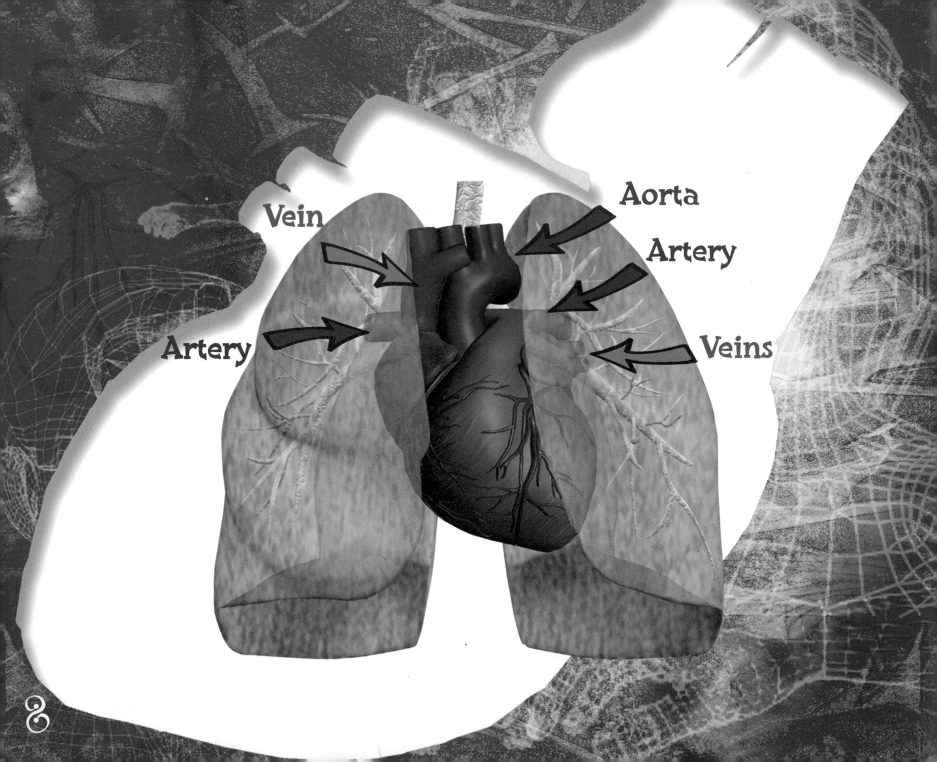

The Journey of Blood

After oxygen is added to your blood, and carbon dioxide is taken away, the blood travels to your heart. Your heart delivers the blood to the rest of your body through tubes called arteries. Once your blood makes its journey through your body, the blood becomes low in oxygen. It then travels back to your heart in tubes called **veins**. The blood is filled with carbon dioxide because it has used up most of its oxygen. Your heart then takes in this weak blood and pumps it to your lungs to be refreshed. The path your blood travels through is called the **circulatory system**.

One half of your heart, the right side, pumps blood to your lungs. In the lungs, the blood is filled with oxygen. Then the blood is returned to the other half of your heart, the left side. From there, it is pumped through arteries to the rest of your body. The oxygen is used and then veins carry the blood, now filled with carbon dioxide, back to the right side of your heart.

Inside the Heart

Your heart has four chambers, or sections, inside it. The top chambers are called the **atria**. The bottom chambers are called **ventricles**. Blood always takes the same route as it travels through the heart. First it goes into the right atrium, then down to the right ventricle. Next it goes to the lungs to pick up oxygen. It comes back in through the left atrium and then goes to the left ventricle. The biggest pump of blood comes when the blood leaves the left ventricle to deliver oxygen to the rest of the body.

When you look at a picture of the heart, the right atrium and the right ventricle are on the left side of the picture.

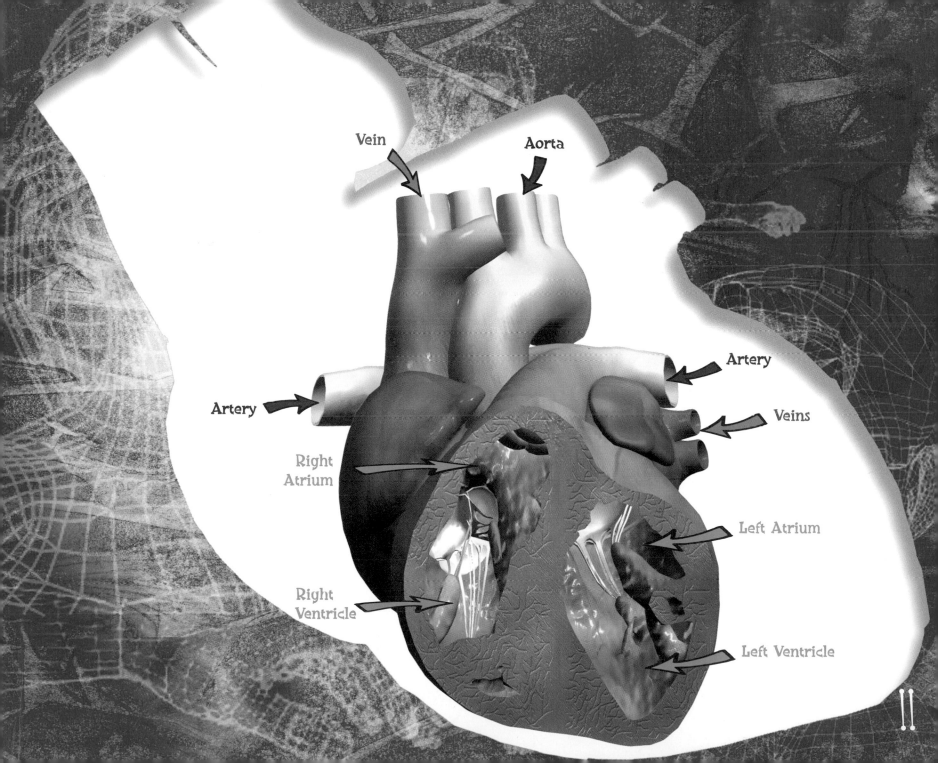

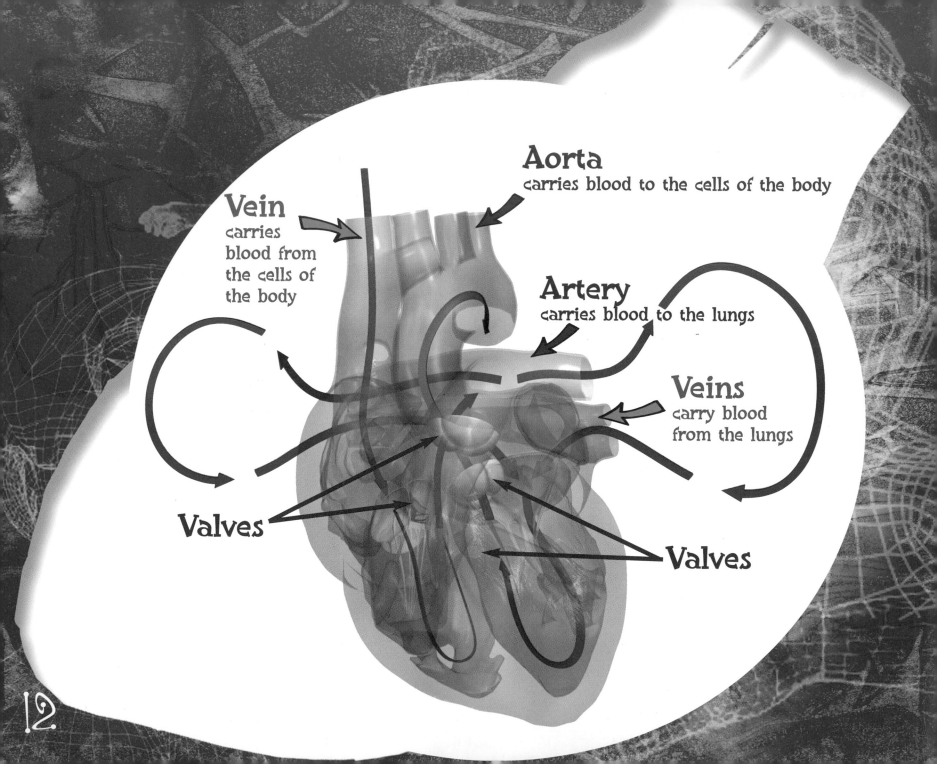

Vein
carries blood from the cells of the body

Aorta
carries blood to the cells of the body

Artery
carries blood to the lungs

Veins
carry blood from the lungs

Valves

Valves

How Does Blood Know Where to Go?

Does blood ever get mixed up and go to the wrong place? No, because blood travels through a one-way system made up of veins and arteries. Veins always bring blood to the heart. Arteries always take blood away from the heart. The biggest artery in your body is called the aorta. It carries blood out of your left ventricle and gets the blood started on its path through your body. Your heart has valves that keep the blood flowing in a one-way direction. The valves open when blood pushes through. Then they close to prevent the blood from going back the wrong way.

Blood travels through your veins on its way to your heart (blue arrows). It travels through your arteries as it goes away from your heart (red arrows). The sound of a heartbeat is caused by the valves of the atria and ventricles closing.

What Is in Blood?

Your blood is made up of tiny **white blood cells** and tiny **red blood cells**. These cells are too small to be seen with your eyes. White blood cells help fight illness. When they travel through your body, they attack germs and disease. This is very important to keep you healthy. Red blood cells carry the oxygen that your body needs. The oxygen makes your blood bright red. Not all of your blood is bright red, though. The blood in your veins is purplish in color because there is not a lot of oxygen in it. The blood in your arteries is the reddest in your body because it carries blood rich in oxygen.

This is an illustration of red blood cells. The shape of red blood cells make them able to travel through narrow spaces like arteries.

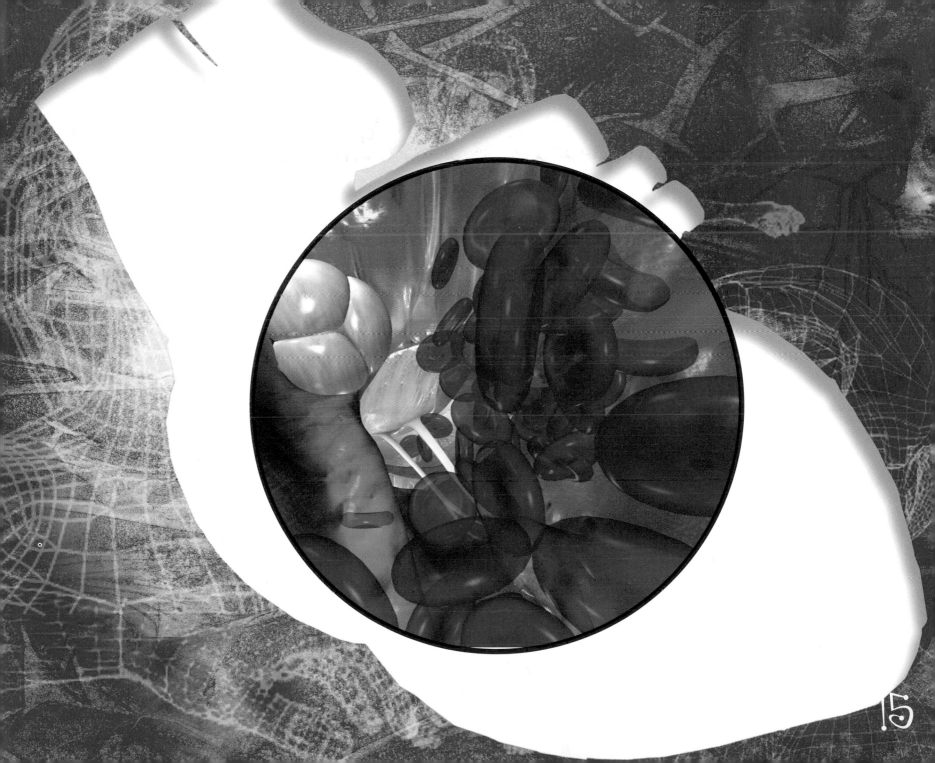

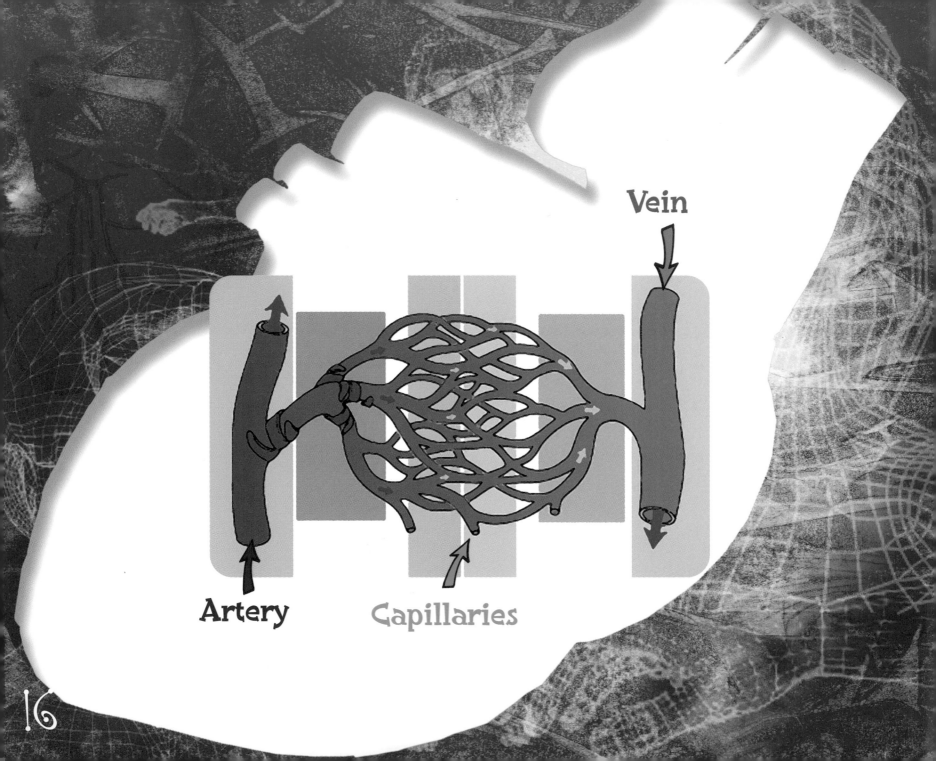

Vein

Artery

Capillaries

16

The End of the Trail

How does the blood in your arteries deliver the oxygen to your little toe? All around your body are tiny tubes called capillaries, which connect arteries with veins. Capillaries are found in your muscles and everywhere that blood travels. The walls of your capillaries are so thin that oxygen can pass right through them. Blood delivers oxygen to your little toe through these capillaries. Then the blood travels back to your heart through a vein.

This picture shows how the tiny capillaries connect the arteries to the veins. The arteries are bright red in color because they carry blood that is rich in oxygen. Veins carry blood that is low in oxygen but full of carbon dioxide. That is why they are a purplish color.

Your Heart Rate

Feel the side of your neck just under your jawbone. This is a place on your body that you can feel to see how fast your heart is beating. The speed at which your heart beats is called your **heart rate**. Your heart rate is faster after you exercise than it is when you are at rest. It beats faster during exercise because your muscles are working harder and need more fuel. Blood always pumps through your arteries at the exact speed of your heart rate. When you visit a doctor's office, you can hear the sound of your heartbeat through a tool called a stethoscope.

If you cannot feel your heart rate on your neck, try touching your wrist with your finger.

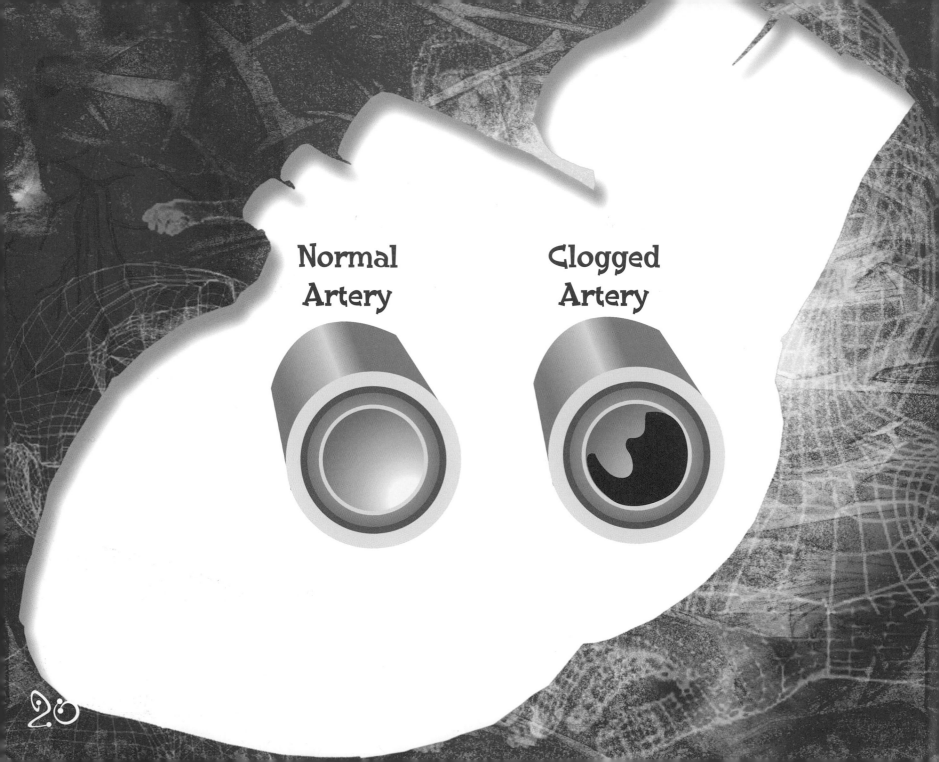

Heart Problems

Sometimes people are born with heart problems, or they might develop them when they get older. Arteries that are too narrow or valves that do not close properly can keep blood from flowing the right way. Heart problems can also be caused by a bad diet and lack of exercise. When people eat foods that are high in fat, the fat can build up in the arteries. Clogged arteries can keep blood from carrying oxygen throughout your body. When oxygen cannot get through your arteries, your heart cannot keep its normal beat. This can cause a sudden and painful heart problem called a **heart attack**.

A normal artery carries blood with oxygen throughout the body. A clogged artery keeps the oxygen-rich blood from reaching the parts of the body and can cause a heart attack.

Taking Care of Your Heart

The best way to keep your heart healthy is to get plenty of exercise and to eat right. The more exercise your body gets, the more oxygen you will bring into your body. Your heart is a muscle, and just like all of your muscles, it works best when it is strong. Exercise makes the heart stronger. Fat usually gets caught only in the arteries of older people, but everyone can benefit from learning to eat right while they are young. A balanced diet of many different foods is best, with fewer fatty foods and lots of fruits and vegetables.

Glossary

artificial heart (ar-tih-FIH-shul HART) A machine that can do the work of a heart.

atria (AY-tree-uh) Heart chambers that take in blood from the body.

carbon dioxide (KAR-bin dy-OK-syd) A gas that the body makes to get rid of waste from energy that was used.

circulatory system (SIR-kyew-lih-tor-ee SIS-tehm) The path that blood travels through the body.

gas (GAS) A substance that is not liquid or solid, has no size or shape of its own, and can expand without limit.

heart attack (HART AH-tak) A sudden and painful problem caused by heart disease, in which the heart stops working properly.

heart rate (HART RAYT) The number of times your heart beats in one minute.

heart transplant (HART TRANZ-plant) An operation that replaces an old heart with a healthy heart in a very sick person.

oxygen (AHK-sih-jin) A gas in air that has no color, taste, or odor and is necessary for people and animals to breathe.

red blood cells (RED BLUD SELZ) Cells that carry oxygen through the body.

veins (VAYNZ) Tubes that carry blood toward the heart.

ventricles (VEN-trih-kuhlz) Chambers of the heart from which blood is pumped to the body.

white blood cells (WHYT BLUD SELZ) Cells that help the body fight illnesses.

23

Index

A

aorta, 13
arteries, 9, 13, 14, 17, 18, 21, 22
artificial heart, 5
atria, 10

C

capillaries, 17
carbon dioxide, 6, 9
circulatory system, 9

E

energy, 5, 6

H

heart attack, 21
heart rate, 18
heart transplant, 5

L

lungs, 6, 9, 10

O

oxygen, 6, 9, 10, 14, 17, 21, 22

R

red blood cells, 14

S

stethoscope, 18

V

veins, 9, 13, 14, 17
ventricles, 10

W

white blood cells, 14

Web Sites

For more information about the heart and circulatory system, check out these Web sites:

http://tqjunior.advanced.org/5777/cir1.htm
http://www.imcpl.lib.in.us/nov_circ.htm
http://www.healthyfridge.org/mainmenu.html
http://tqjunior.advanced.org/5407